Death Is a Serious Business

Death Is a Serious Business
"A Book about Life"

By

Skip Quant

ISBN: 978-0-578-00828-8

Table of Contents

Introduction

There are two things that all of you reading this book have in common... The first is you are all living right now as you read this book. The second is you will all die after you finish the book. Hopefully not immediately after you finish it!

I had a chemistry teacher in junior high school that had a favorite trick he liked to play on each new class. He would put a small amount of dry ice in a beaker of colored water and then he would dramatically say to the unsuspecting class, "I'm going to drink this and after I drink it, I'm going to die!" As the astonished class watched him drink the smoking beverage, he would then say, "Well, I didn't die before I drank it, so I guess I'll die afterwards." Much relieved, the entire class got the point. The simple fact remains, sometime in the future we are all going to die. Some will die sooner, others later. I personally hope for later.

We have all had the gripping experience of thinking about our own death from time to time. Sheer terror and anxiety come over us as we come to the stark realization that we cannot escape death. It is a brief but sobering moment similar to a panic attack. We've all had them.

In the next six chapters, you will read not only about death, but moreover, about life. Death is simply the absence of life as we know it. Very little is known about death except the obvious... It is very, very permanent. Or is it?

Read on and learn a little about death, and a lot about life...

Chapter One

In The Beginning

The first three words of the Bible are..."In the beginning" Genesis 1:1 The last word of the Bible is found in Revelation 22:21. It reads "Amen" That is, of course, if you don't count "The End" at the bottom of the page. Ironically, "Amen" is usually the last word said at someone's funeral. I guess "The End" might be too melodramatic for the family. In my Bible, I have scratched through the words "The End" simply because it isn't the end. In reality it's the beginning...

Let me say at this point, this is <u>not</u> a book about religion. However, it does have some religious overtones. Death is indeed a serious business and very little is known about the hereafter. Death is mostly an unknown. The main example of life after death we have is found in the bible. The death and resurrection of Jesus Christ is the most well known example and I think, for a good reason. The Bible has dozens of scriptures regarding death and the dead. There are two categories of death, physical and spiritual. Like wise, there are two categories of life, physical and spiritual. Most people relate to this by subscribing to the concepts of Heaven and Earth and Heaven and Hell. We all live on earth. (No, women aren't really from Venus and men aren't really from Mars.) Most Judeo-Christians believe in Heaven and Hell. If you live your life as a good person, you get to go to Heaven as your reward. Conversely, if you were a bad person, you must go to Hell. Some religions throw in "Purgatory" so once you've "done your time", you finally get to go to Heaven and be with some of your relatives. These concepts are promoted in most Christian churches today with a few minor variations. That is what most fundamental Christians believe from the time they can remember... Heaven and Hell, good and evil... Fascinating! In the book of Ecclesiastes Chapter 9 verse 5 we read "For the living know that they shall die: but the dead know not any thing..." Another interesting scripture is found in John 3:13 which reads "No man hath ascended up to Heaven, but he that came down from Heaven, even the son of man which is in Heaven." In fact, there are many scriptures that refer to death simply as sleep. While I will let the evangelists debate each other on the subjects of Heaven and Hell, I remain focused on one certain thing, death. There is an old Greek proverb that says ***"Nothing is more certain than death and nothing more uncertain than the hour of death."*** A more modern quote ***is " Death is nature's way of telling you to slow down."***

The mortality tables used in computing life insurance premiums are amazingly accurate. They are very accurate and their actuaries are second only to the odds makers in Las Vegas! But the mortality rate remains the same... One death per person!

Chapter 2

A Matter of Life and Death

How many times have we heard someone say, "It's an emergency, it's a matter of life and death!" That is supposed to make it the very top priority. Nobody would deny another person that kind of emergency, would they? Does that mean that someone is dying or about to? Sometimes it may be just an excuse to get to use the payphone right away. Sincere or not, it gets people's attention for certain. If it's a matter of life and death, shouldn't we really say a matter of life <u>or</u> death? Just being picky here...

Earlier, we described death as the absence of life <u>as we know it</u>. Yes, as we know it. How do you know it? What is life to you? Life is our most precious gift. It is a gift from God to each of us. We are commanded to love one another. Another commandment says "Thou Shalt Not Kill." This seems to make perfect sense to me... How about you? Why then do some people decide to end their own lives? The most precious gift we have is not to be thrown away. Let's say that the Prize Patrol shows up at your door with a check for ten million dollars. You have just been named this year's winner of the big sweepstakes. As they present you with the ten million dollar check and are taking your picture, you decide to just tear up the check and throw it away. Is that likely? I doubt it. Yet, some people decide to end their own lives. They throw away their greatest gift. As my son Andrew said when he was just two years old, "Where there's life there's hope". I'm sure he must have heard that somewhere, but I've never been able to find out where. He did grow up to be a pretty smart fellow! It's amazing that such a young person could learn so early to place such great value on life and hope. It is my hope that many people both young and old will read this book and learn from it. It's been said, "Live and learn", maybe we should say "Continue to live and continue to learn". I've always said that an "expert" is someone who has ceased learning in his or her field of endeavor. We are never too old to stop learning. Amazingly, we begin to learn at a very early age. I have heard of children as young as two years old with an advanced vocabulary. Some young children have learned to play musical instruments before they enter kindergarten. Our potential as human beings is truly a mystery. Our capacity to learn is astounding. It is very important that we learn as much as possible, whenever possible. Our quality of life is dependant upon how much we learn. Learning is a life long process, but it begins at a very early age. It begins with what I call "The Learning Years"...

Chapter 3

The Learning Years

I like to think of life as I have labeled the chapters of this book. It starts with the beginning and ends with the end. In between we have the big three phases of life, and after all, this is a book about life! The big three as I like to call them are: The Learning Years, The Earning Years, and The Yearning Years. If we learn in our learning years and we earn in our earning years, then we can truly enjoy our yearning years. All of the above require taking each period of our life very seriously. Too many people just go through life, taking it and everything associated with it for granted. When the end starts looming on the horizon, all of a sudden everything becomes more important, more urgent. The big problem with that is... time is up! Life flies by in no time at all. Before too long we begin to relate to our parents when they were our age. All of a sudden we feel really old. I remember when I turned twenty one, a significant milestone in my life. My father was twenty one when I was born. I am now sixty years old and I am now older than my father was when I married my beautiful bride, Michelle, in 1982. My father, Harold Atwell Quant died on April 14, 2005 at the age of seventy eight. I am certain that if and when I am afforded seventy eight years, I will no doubt recall that I would be the same age as my father was when he died. The old clock on the wall doesn't slow down for anybody. We can't afford to wait until it's too late to learn, earn, or yearn.

Of all the phases of life, perhaps the most important is the learning years. The learning years will probably determine how much we earn and subsequently, yearn. Although learning is a life long process, it is vital that we begin to learn as soon as possible. My children are still in their learning years, but are now entering their earning years. Two have graduated from college. My youngest will graduate in 2010. I am very proud that all three of my children, Andrew; Angela; and Emily, made National Honor Society in High School. They are three very smart children. No brag, just fact. They were blessed with reasonably intelligent parents, mostly on their mother's side, of course! I credit the reason they have learned so well to the fact that Michelle started reading to them at a very early age. Hours upon hours were spent reading "Pat the Bunny". I think I actually have it memorized! My favorite part was "Daddy's scratchy face". Early reading to a child builds their interest in reading which greatly enhances their ability to learn. Not only does it enhance their learning ability, it also helps them develop good self esteem and confidence. A young mother once commented to me that she didn't read to her child because she was not a very good reader. My comment in return was, "Your child won't know and by the time she figures it out, you will have greatly increased your reading skills through practice!"

I once worked with a man who although not a great salesman, was a very hard worker. He got the job done by hard work alone. We'll call him Joe. Each time Joe had a sales letter to write, he would ask me to do it for him. As his manager, I felt Joe should write his own letters and I told him so. However, I agreed to review and edit his sales letters before he mailed them. His letters were not good. In fact, they were terrible. Filled with typographical errors and poor grammar, they would have been an embarrassment to the company if sent out unedited. One day I suggested to Joe that he take some remedial courses in English and maybe even a few writing courses. He bristled at the suggestion and replied, "Go to college at my age? "Do you know how old I would be by the time I graduated?" I said, "Joe, how old will you be in four years if you don't go to college?" Joe was in his late forties at the time and had never attended college. I'm pleased to say that Joe took my admonition to heart and although he didn't attain a degree, he is now quite capable of sending well written letters. He decided to not stop learning! When you couple confidence with competence and throw in a strong work ethic, you have a good recipe for success. Success in life is more than just a fat paycheck and a nice house with a new car in the driveway. A wise man once said, "Success isn't measured by what you have, but rather by your lack of wants". The road to success begins with the learning years. It is never too late to learn in any of your years. Several famous people have attained college degrees later in life. The late actress, Butterfly McQueen, who played in Gone with the Wind, graduated with her Bachelors degree in her seventies. One of my all time favorite professional football players, Emmitt Smith, finished his college education while playing for the Dallas Cowboys. The Cowboys had already won a Super Bowl with Smith as the star running back. I'd say he successfully combined his learning years with his earning years! Emmitt Smith retired after breaking Walter Payton's all time rushing record in the National Football League. He still has his degree...

The road to success in life truly starts with the learning years. And while it's never too late for learning, the same cannot be said of the earning years, that phase usually has a window of opportunity. Prepare yourself with learning and obtaining a good education, because before you know it, you are entering "The Earning Years".

Chapter 4

The Earning Years

As I stated in the previous chapter, "The Learning Years", it is never too late to be learning. In fact, the most successful people continue to learn as much as possible all of their lives. The earning years are somewhat different in that there is usually a window of opportunity. While this is not always the case, it is largely true for most people. Some people who start their own businesses and have their children successfully take over the day to day operations may continue to reap financial benefits many years after they retire. But by and large, the vast majority of us have to work for a living.

I like to say that there are two sources of income. Man at work and money at work. Man typically works eight hours a day, five days a week, and takes two weeks vacation a year. Man can become unemployed, get sick, become disabled, or even die. Man usually works from ages twenty one to sixty five, then retires and dies. I still firmly believe that retirement is the leading cause of death in America! Don't let yourself atrophy. Stay out of that rocking chair! Get a hobby, do volunteer work, deliver "Meals on Wheels", but don't just sit around waiting to die, because you will! That pretty well sums up man at work. It is best to position yourself to understand the concept of money at work as soon as possible.

Unlike man at work, money at work doesn't become unemployed, disabled or die. Money works twenty four hours a day, seven days a week, three hundred sixty five days a year. It never calls in sick or takes vacation. Best of all... It doesn't die! It keeps working for man even after he dies. Get money working for you as soon as possible because there will probably come a time when you can no longer work for money. As I stated earlier, when time is up, it's too late to start over or try again. As the old saying goes, "Life is not a dress rehearsal". Enjoy your moments in the sun because "sundown" is right around the corner. Before you know it, just like winter, the days are getting shorter.

My Story...

You may be wondering what qualifies me to write this book, a book about life. First, I have experienced the learning years, the earning years, and am now in my yearning years. As I stated earlier, I am sixty years old and I retired from business at age fifty one as a multi-millionaire, no brag, just fact. *(We say that a lot in Texas. Being from Texas, we have lots of sayings that we like to use. For example, never ask a man if he's from Texas, if he is, he'll tell you. If he's not, there's no need to embarrass him!)*

I quit high school on my seventeenth birthday and enlisted in the United States Marine Corps. I will never forget checking out with each of my teachers from my senior class. My English teacher (I can't remember her name) asked me what I was going to do. I told her I was joining the Marines. She said, "Marines, huh? Well, they'll either make you or break you!" She was right! Little did either of us know just how right she would prove to be... I sure wish I could remember her name!

On September 15, 1965 I became Private Quant, a proud member of Platoon 280 at the Marine Corps Recruit Depot at Parris Island, South Carolina. My Drill Instructors were SSGT. Richard Handley; Sgt. Roscoe Burgoyne; and Corporal Marion Davis. In September 1966 I was sent to Vietnam and I later went on R&R to Taipei with SSGT. Roscoe Burgoyne, we remained lifelong friends. Just before his death in 2000, Roscoe's daughter sent me an e-mail informing me that her father was dying. She asked if I could write him a letter as my letters and phone calls had meant so much to him over the years. I wrote a letter that day and e-mailed it immediately. In the letter, I thanked him for taking a young 17 year old "boy" and transforming him into not just a man, but a United States Marine. I told him that everything that I had achieved in life was due to my being in the Marine Corps and he was the one that put me on a rock solid foundation. His daughter wrote to inform me that Roscoe had time to read my letter. After reading it, he smiled and quietly passed away shortly thereafter. I was deeply touched by his death and was honored that we remained friends until the very end.

After returning from Vietnam, I was assigned to the Marine Barracks in Washington, D.C. as member of Ceremonial Guard Company. During that time, I served as the Platoon Sergeant of 2nd Platoon. My Commanding Officer was Major Frank Breth. Frank retired as Brigadier General and we remained in close contact until his death in December of 2003. My Platoon Commander was Lt. Frank M. Izenour, Jr. the son of Major General Frank M. Izenour, Sr. in the United States Army. Lt. Izenour and I were selected to be the Officer and NCO in charge of the Marine detail in the Honor Guard for the funeral of former President Dwight D. Eisenhower. Soon, Lt. Izenour was promoted to Captain and became the Executive Officer to

Major Breth. My new Platoon Commander was 1st Lt. Peter Pace who had just returned from Vietnam. Peter Pace was a very bright and likable officer who had graduated from the Naval Academy at Annapolis. I recall one night at Camp David while I was Commander of Guard and Lt. Pace was the Officer of the day. Lt. Pace came by the guard house for a visit and we spent a long time talking over coffee. I was telling Lt. Pace that I was getting out of the Marine Corps very soon and thought that he should too. I told him that anyone as sharp and intelligent as him should not waste his time in the military, but get out and become the President of some big company. He was sharp as a tack and I told him he could make a lot more money in business than he would ever see in the Marine Corps. Lt. Pace seemed to ponder his thoughts for a moment then explained that he had planned to make a career out of the Marine Corps, but appreciated my input. I walked away thinking "He'll probably become a General someday..." As I write this book, General Peter Pace is retired as the 16th Chairman of the Joint Chiefs of Staff, the first Marine to hold that position. Prior to becoming Chairman, he was the Vice Chairman of the Joint Chiefs of Staff. In achieving these positions as the highest ranking military man in America, he is also the highest ranking Marine in the history of the Marine Corps. He jokingly claims he was "Quant Trained". I sure do wish I could remember that English teachers name...

General Pace and I remain good friends to this day. My wife and I attended his swearing in ceremony on September 30, 2005 at Fort Myer and spent the rest of the day and much of the evening with him and his family. In October, 2007 I attended his retirement ceremony also held at Fort Myer. In 2005, I attended an 8th & I reunion in Washington, D.C. After the event, Pete and Lynne Pace joined me for a visit in my hotel suite. Pete presented me with the cufflinks he was wearing with his uniform. He mentioned that he had five sets made. One he was keeping for himself, one was for his wife, one for his son Pete Jr. and one for Tiffany, his daughter. I was deeply honored that he gave the fifth pair to me.

As I told Roscoe Burgoyne in my final letter to him, I owe everything that I have achieved to the Marine Corps. I treasure my friendships and stay in close contact with Marines with whom I served. Men like General Peter Pace, Colonel Sheldon "Jim" Bathurst, and the late Brig. Gen. Frank Breth. I also stay in touch with Corporal Rich Porter, Sgt Terry Shannon and Sgt. Ernie Richardson, all former 8th & I Marines that served with me during 1968-1970. Frank M. Izenour Jr. passed away from a massive heart attack in December 1988 at the age of forty six. Frank had just retired six months earlier as a Lt. Col in the Marine Corps. He left behind a widow, Susan, six year old son Chris, and four year old daughter Katy. Upon hearing the news of his untimely death, I realized that there would be nobody to tell his children of his "Glory Days" at the Marine Barracks at 8th & I Streets, Washington, D.C. I took it upon myself to accomplish this task. It took several months, but I managed to write a brief book outlining our times at 8th & I. Upon receiving the book, Susan called to thank me and ask for one additional copy. I sent her another copy the next day. Little did I know at that time that Frank's six year old son, Chris, would grow up treasuring that book about his Dad. In May 2004, I had the honor to be invited to West Point to stand in for Frank Izenour and attend the graduation of his son Chris Izenour and pin his gold Lieutenants bars on him. The same gold bars that were pinned on his grandfather, the late Major General Frank M. Izenour Sr. at his West Point graduation in 1938. The final chapter of this book contains a copy Of "Lest we Forget" dedicated to the late Lt. Colonel Frank M. Izenour, Jr. His two children are now my Godchildren.

I am also deeply honored to have become acquainted with several recipients of the Congressional Medal of Honor. Colonel H.C. "Barney" Barnum with whom I served on General Walt's staff remains a good friend. I have received challenge coins from 17 recipients of the Medal of Honor and was presented with a book of the Congressional Medal of Honor by recipients, Barney Barnum, Donald "Doc" Ballard and Bob O'Malley when they visited me at my ranch in August 2004. I continue to treasure these relationships to this day. Colonel Roger H.C. Donlon, the first Medal of Honor recipient in Vietnam presented me with an autographed copy of his book "Beyond Nam Dong". Roger was kind enough to write a touching inscription along with his autograph. Roger Donlon is an amazing man with an amazing wife, Norma. Their words of life which are inscribed on his wedding band sum up their combined philosophy of life.

> ***What we are is God's gift to us...***
> ***What we become is our gift to God...***

The Marines taught me many things... Courage, Honor, and Commitment. For sure, discipline. I learned that hard work, competence coupled with confidence, was a winning combination. I was released from the Marine Corps with an Honorable discharge in 1971. I was about to enter my earning years...

In 1970, I joined Dun & Bradstreet, Commercial Collection Division in San Jose, California. . The business world was very different from the Marine Corps; however, I still thought and acted like a combat Marine. I didn't sell prospects; I attacked them with the tenacity of a bulldog, just like the Marine Corps mascot! I attacked enough of them that I won three Presidential Citations, the highest award Dun & Bradstreet gives for sales excellence. The rewards were trips to the Bahamas and then to St. Maartin.

After 11 years I left D&B and advanced through a few senior level executive positions in the collection agency business. I joined Telecredit Collection Service in 1982 and went from Account Executive to President of the company in thirteen months. Telecredit was later acquired by Equifax in 1990.

In 1981, my entire life changed... I was living in Marina Del Rey, California, living the good life. So I thought. Actually, I was miserable. A failed marriage had left me flat broke and lonely. I was on the verge of becoming homeless. I spent two months sleeping in my car. I was miserable. Most of the women I dated were shallow and were only interested in what you could do for them. I prayed for God to send me just one good woman that I could really truly love...

On January 21, 1981, he dispatched Michelle Bumpers, a beautiful 25 year old girl from Texas, to be my wife. She came in for a job interview and the rest is history! (I'll spare you poor readers most of the history as I realize it is only of interest to me.) To make a long story short, one morning Michelle drove down from Pasadena to meet me for breakfast. Over breakfast, I told her what our lives would be like from now on. I said. "We're going to get married, move back to Texas, have a bunch of kids, buy a ranch and put down roots." She said, "Okay", and that's exactly what we did!

We married on June 27, 1982. Our son Andrew was born in October 1983, Angela was born in August 1985, and our wonderful little surprise, Emily born in October 1988.

In June, 1986, I joined a large agency called FCA. I soon became a Vice President with national sales responsibility. After four years, the founding family patriarch decided to sell the family's interest. I decided to sell mine as well and start my own company, Creditwatch, Inc. My decision proved to be a good one as the company grew and prospered over the next ten years.

Over ten years, I took out several million dollars in salary, bonus, and perquisites. Always shining the spotlight on my employees, the reflection back on me seemed to continually magnify ten fold. We were blessed with some fabulous employees who started with me and stayed with me the full ten years. People like Scott McIntosh, Kyra Neff, Debbie Tompkins, John Golden, Mike Shelton and

Annegret Werle helped make the company such a great success. John Golden is a retired Special Agent, United States Secret Service. John is also my best friend and a throw back to my Marine Corps days. John and I served in 1968-69 at Camp David under President's Johnson and Nixon. I was Commander of the Guard and John was a member of the PPD, Presidential Protection Detail. We had lost track of each other until 1994 when a coincidental meeting with some other Secret Service Agents reunited us. John retired from the Secret Service in 1995 and shortly thereafter joined Creditwatch, Inc. as Vice President of Security.

In March of 2000, I sold Creditwatch, Inc. to a Bank One led investor group for several million dollars. I received most of the money up front, but was owed $750,000 over the next five years. The monthly sum of $12,500 was to be paid on the 15th of every month until the last payment was made on February 15, 2005. This date proved to be important as you will soon see.

In October 1997, I purchased a 168 acre ranch in Burleson, Texas for the sum of $400,000. The ranch had been owned by the same family since 1946 and they were anxious to sell. So anxious, in fact, that they agreed to give me all the mineral rights that they owned. They owned 100%.

I spent a lot of time clearing brush and doing some hard manual labor to clean up the ranch, it had fallen into a state of complete disrepair as the family had rented out the property for the past several years.

When I sold the company in March 2000, I paid off the mortgage on the land. My wife and I decided in 1999 to build a large colonial style mansion on the ranch and in May 2000, we moved in.

In early 2004 I started getting phone calls from various land agents who wanted to me to lease my mineral rights for oil and gas exploration. I recalled the words of the family that sold me the land when I asked them for all the mineral rights, *"We don't mind giving up the mineral rights, we've been out here since 1946, if there was any oil out here, we'd have found it by now."* Well... (Pardon the pun) maybe no oil, but by now I had been hearing about a massive gas formation called the Barnett Shale. It just happens to lie right underneath my ranch! It's a blanket formation spread over ten counties with trillions of cubic feet of natural gas. Our well started pumping gas to market on February 15, 2005, the last day of my Creditwatch income. How is that for timing? We now have five wells either on our land or in our pool that are paying us royalties. We are now making more income from these royalties than I earned as President of Creditwatch. Money is now working for me, not the other way around! As the late Eddie Childs, legendary Texas oil man and former owner of the Texas Rangers baseball team once said, *"If you don't have an oil well, get one!"*

The late billionaire J. Paul Getty said it best when asked for his secret to success. His reply was *"Rise early, work hard, strike oil!"*

Of course, there is an element of luck involved... My definition of luck is simple. Luck is good planning, carefully executed. I have also found that the harder I worked, the luckier I got! Let's be honest, luck is for rabbits. Look at the symbol of luck, a rabbit's foot. It didn't do the rabbit any good!

My business was not a glamorous or glorified one. No Mother raises her son to be a bill collector. A collection agency seems an unlikely place to make a small fortune. A bill collector! I might just as well have been a garbage collector, like what's his name... Wayne Huizinga! You see my point. No matter what your field of endeavor, just do your very best at it. In Ecclesiastes 9:10 you will read the following *"Whatsoever they hand findeth to do, do it with all thy might..."*

In 1994, I was privileged to be the keynote speaker at Texas A&M University's graduation ceremony of the Business School. In my speech, I used the aforementioned scripture in explaining the importance of doing your very best regardless of which career path you may choose. I used the example of two men in Arlington, Texas who flip hamburgers for a living. They both flip burgers for a living, they both flip them the same way every time and they both flip them all day long. The first man works at McDonald's, he makes minimum wage. The second man is named Al. Al makes a lot of money. If you're ever in Arlington, Texas at lunch time, you have many choices for lunch. But if you want a world class burger, go to Al's Hamburgers on N. Collins St. But, be sure to get there early, because the line goes around the corner. There are plenty of McDonald's...

What makes the difference? The answer is: "Al". He flips them with all his might and he uses a circa 1950's grill and French fries made fresh daily. No, make that hourly. Al now has the whole family involved with the burger production company. He is one of those who will retire and still receive a nice income while his family continues to run the day to day operation. Al is now entering his yearning years.

Maximize your opportunities in your earning years and you will be well positioned to enjoy what may be the happiest time of your life... The Yearning Years.

Chapter 5

The Yearning Years

"Yearning". Webster defines it as: 1. A deep longing. The root word is Yearn. It is defined as: 1.To have a strong or deep desire; to long. 2. To feel deep pity, sympathy, or tenderness.

What will you be longing for in your retirement?

Will it be a deep longing to travel to far away places that you've always wanted to visit but didn't have the time or money until now? Perhaps you'll think about climbing the Great Wall of China with your beloved spouse by your side. Maybe you imagine seeing Paris for the first time with your grandchildren. A Caribbean cruise with your entire family might also be nice.

Yearning for others may simply be the sight of the mailman. Hopefully he will have your Social Security check in his mail bag today so you can finally buy a few groceries and keep the electricity on for another month. Perhaps you will yearn for the "Meals on Wheels" volunteer to appear at your door. What will it be? Dining at a fine outdoor bistro with your grandchildren in Paris, or "Meals on Wheels"? You decide. But decide now, because you only get one shot at the duck, then it flies away and doesn't come back to give you a second shot. Ducks are funny that way. So is life.

Your yearning might consist of that feeling of deep pity, sympathy, or tenderness. Perhaps a sibling who didn't learn, or earn as they should have in their appropriate years needs to borrow money, again. What yearning is that for you? What about Sympathy? Sympathy doesn't buy food or clothing. Neither does pity. You may just turn a blind eye and say, "I'm sorry for the position you're in, but you had the same choices to make as I did." You may not come right out and say it, but you certainly are thinking it. What if you're the one who needs the pity, sympathy or tenderness?

I recently read about some senior citizens living on dog food. It is very sad indeed to think about someone who has become that forlorn. Let's see, can we afford Alpo this week or do we have to settle for Mighty Dog again?

Every time I see a homeless person I can't help but wonder to myself, what was there life like? Did they have a family? Where is their family now? Are they aware of his or her plight? Do they care? I can't come up with answers on my own short of stopping to ask the homeless person. I just haven't been able to bring myself to do that yet. I don't know if I would get an honest answer anyway. Not all homeless people are alcoholics, although many of them are. Yearning still applies to them as well. Their yearning is quite different as is their level of priority and needs. A warm shelter on cold winter night may be all they're yearning for at that moment.

Most people would prefer to yearn for a visit from their children or grandchildren, or both. Yearning for the celebration of a 50th wedding anniversary and still being as much in love as the day you wed. Oh the choices we make during our lives! What leads us to yearn? To live out our golden years in comfort and security without any fears or wants is everyone's desire. One need not be a millionaire to have wonderful yearning years. Remember, success isn't measured by what you have, but rather by your lack of wants.

I've known quite a few rich people who aren't very happy and are by no means successful. Conversely, I know a few people of very meager means who are successful and quite content with their lives and "want" for nothing. A good family is the foundation for success. My son is married to a very nice young lady and they are expecting their first child. He recently asked me what the secret to having wealth was... My reply was "Either stay single or stay married." Seriously, a good spouse can make all the difference when it comes to enjoying your success and yearning years. I credit much of my success and happiness to my wife, Michelle, for being such a resilient and strong woman who remains strongly committed to our marriage.

All of the things I have written about are things that I have experienced in my life. The learning years, the earning years, and the yearning years are all things that I have personally experienced. Needless to say, I have not yet experienced "The end". So, to put it in "angelic" terms, I'm going to have to "wing it".

We all know the day will come. We just don't know how, when or where. Actually, some do know how. I always talk about my great, great, great grandfather. He was an old Indian fighter. (The young ones used to beat the tar out of him.) Seriously, he was a psychic. He knew the exact day and how he was going to die. How? The judge told him!

If death is inevitable, and it is, we might as well not go quietly into that good night.

The final chapter of this book is simply relative to the final stage of life. I aptly call it, The End...

Chapter 6

The End

It's that time. We all meet our end. I think most of us would like to just go to sleep and pass quietly without actually knowing it. This type of death experience is the most desirable, preferably sometime in our late nineties. The late comedian George Burns was booked into the London palladium for his one hundredth birthday. The announcement was made when he was ninety five. He loved to joke about it, saying, "Get your tickets early, I understand it's a sellout"! Obviously, the booking announcement was just a marvelous publicity stunt to draw attention to the fact that George Burns was still working at the ripe old age of ninety five. However, George did live to see his one hundredth birthday! He died shortly thereafter... What a life! He continued in his earning years until he died.

Another late actor, George Sanders, left a rather bizarre suicide note. It read simply "I'm bored". He died on April 25, 1972 in Barcelona, Spain. Bored? Gee, he could have gone to a bullfight if he was bored... Oh well, too late now.

The apostle Paul wrote in his letter to the Corinthians, "O death, where is thy sting". (1Corinthians 15:55) In fact, there are over one hundred scriptures in the Bible that deal with death and dying. I would recommend anyone read them for a better understanding of the subject and maybe even a little inspiration. For those of you who are spiritually inclined, I also recommend a very good pamphlet published by the United Church of God titled "What Happens after Death". This pamphlet is free of charge and can be obtained on their website **www.ucg.org**. There is no cost or obligation.

Causes of Death:

According to the National Vital Statistics Reports Vol. 53 No. 17 dated March 7, 2005 the leading cause of death is diseases of the heart, responsible for 28.9 % of total deaths. This is a fact.

Here's my thought on the subject...

For those of you who watch what you eat, here's the final word on nutrition and health. It's a relief to know the truth after all those conflicting nutritional studies.

1. The Japanese eat very little fat and suffer fewer heart attacks than Americans.
2. The Mexicans eat a lot of fat and suffer fewer heart attacks than Americans.
3. The Chinese drink very little red wine and suffer fewer heart attacks than Americans.
4. The Italians drink a lot of red wine and suffer fewer heart attacks than Americans.
5. The Germans drink a lot of beer and eat lots of sausages and fats and suffer fewer heart attacks than Americans.

CONCLUSION: Eat and drink what you like.
Speaking English is apparently what kills you!

There is a long list of famous people who died on or before the age of fifty. My personal favorite was that gallant swashbuckler, Errol Flynn. Flynn was born on June 20th, 1909 and died on October 14th, 1959 of heart failure. He was barely fifty years old, although he looked much older. Ironically, Flynn's only son, Sean, would not live to see his thirtieth birthday. He died in Vietnam while serving as a civilian photojournalist.

Success or fame is no guarantee of longevity. There is a long list of people who died young or in their middle age years. We had an interesting trivia game we would play on long road trips in the car. We would try to name all the people who died in plane crashes. Names quickly sprang to mind like, Ricky Nelson, Audie Murphy, Rocky Marciano, Patsy Cline, Buddy Holly, Richey Valens, The Big Bopper, etc. At last count we had named almost one hundred famous people who died in plane crashes.

Some celebrities have enjoyed a very long life. George Burns and Bob Hope both lived to see their one hundredth birthdays. Former President Ronald Reagan lived to be ninety three. Mike Wallace of CBS "60 Minutes" fame is currently near 90, although he looks much younger.

Death is not a respecter of persons. James Dean was in his twenties when an automobile accident claimed his young life. Several young actors have died before their fiftieth birthdays. As I said, death is no respecter of persons and success or fame is no guarantee of longevity.

In Hollywood there is an old axiom, "They always die in three's". Don Knotts, Darren McGaven, and Dennis Weaver all died within forty eight hours of each other. Perhaps they don't always die in threes, these famous folks, but it does seem to draw more attention to their individual passing.

Another old axiom is "Nobody lives longer than a rich relative" I always think of Rose Kennedy when I hear this one. I think Mrs. Kennedy was one hundred and four years old when she died. If this axiom is true, then Bill Gates will easily surpass Shirechiyo Izumi as the oldest man in the world at age one hundred and twenty!

The Bible (Psalm 90:10) gives man an age of "three score and ten" or seventy years. According to U.S. Government statistics, the average life span in America today is seventy seven and one half years. How old will you live to be? Will you see one hundred like George Burns and Bob Hope? Will you die young like Elvis Presley, Ricky Nelson and James Dean? You really don't know.

What will it be for you? A plane crash? A car accident? A heart attack? A stroke? Diabetes? Cancer? A drug overdose? You don't really get a choice, do you? Not unless you decide to commit suicide and I've already addressed that subject as not being an option. Never throw away God's greatest gift to you!

Let's face it. We really don't have a choice as to the method or time of our demise. The bottom line is: **Prepare for it now**. Death can come like thief in the night, unsuspected and unexpected. How do you prepare for it? There are several things that you can do regardless of your age or present health condition. The first thing is make sure you have a current will. If you die "intestate", (without a will), the State in which you reside writes one for you and it may not be according to your wishes. I also recommend you buy as much life insurance as you can comfortably afford. A minimum of ten times your annual income is a good start. Even if you buy term insurance, get all you can afford now and convert it to permanent insurance later. Once you get too old or sick, you'll wish you had done it when you were young and healthy. No widow ever complained that her husband left her too much life insurance. There are plenty of widows who had to sell their home, take their children out of private schools and get jobs, or worse, second jobs to make ends meet. If you truly love your loved ones, buy them all the life insurance you can afford. Remember, it has to last them the rest of their lives.

Another recommendation is to write your own obituary. I wrote mine and what an eye opener it was! Write yours and tell me a tear doesn't come to your eye. A good time to do this by the way is just before you buy life insurance!

When the end comes is different for all of us. Some die instantly, others may linger for weeks, months, or even years. My father died on April 14th, 2005 from Parkinson's disease. He was in Hospice care for three weeks before he died.

Hospice care is for terminally ill people with six months or less to live. As stated by Dr. Elisabeth Kubler Ross, the five stages of grief that most people go through are:

1. Denial and Isolation
2. Anger
3. Bargaining
4. Depression
5. Acceptance.

It is critical for the patient to come to acceptance. Often people get stuck in one of the first four stages. That makes things worse on all parties concerned. I know a man who died of cancer in Hospice care without ever leaving the denial stage. The wonderful people who work in Hospices are trained in helping the families cope with their impending loss. They actually tell the loved ones to give the dying their permission to die. This helps the dying person with the acceptance stage.

When the end comes, no one is absolutely sure of what happens. Many people who have had "near death" experiences tell of seeing a white light or a tunnel. Some claim to have actually talked with God who told them it was not their time yet. Personally, I can neither confirm nor deny such claims. Nor do I care to rely upon them as factual. Death is an unknown, life is a known. What I want everyone who reads this book to understand is that we must deal with the known, not the unknown.

What I do know is that we will all find out what happens after death. If what happens after death is predicated upon what we did in life, then the answer is simple. **Live your life as if every day was your last**. Savor every bite of food as if it were your last meal. Treasure every moment with your loved ones as if it were your last. You never know, it just may be your last...

Live your life as if every day was your last.
I believe that repetition is the best form of emphasis.
Live your life as if every day was your last.
Because before you know it, it is...

The End

Lieutenant Colonel Frank M. Izenour, Jr.

United States Marine Corps

1942–1988

Lest we forget...

By

Skip Quant

March 11, 1990

Revised March, 2009

The news of the assassination of Senator Robert F. Kennedy was the headline for that day in June 1968 as I arrived for duty at the Marine Barracks at 8th & I Streets, SE in Washington, D.C.

The officer of the day was Captain Charles Robb, Adjutant of the Post and later the son-in-law of President Lyndon B. Johnson. Chuck Robb later became a U.S. Senator and the Governor of Virginia.

The Commanding Officer was Colonel Joseph C. Fegan, but was soon replaced by Colonel Paul G. Graham, who later became a Brigadier General and after his retirement was elected as the Mayor of Oceanside, California.

I started my tour at 8th & I as the driver and bodyguard for General Lewis W. Walt, Assistant Commandant of the Marine Corps. My immediate supervisor was Major Carl Mundy (later General Carl Mundy, 30th CMC) and Captain Harvey "Barney" Barnum (Retired as Colonel) recipient of the Congressional Medal of Honor. Within six months my security clearance was approved and I was transferred to Ceremonial Guard Company, 2nd Platoon. The Platoon Leader was Lt. Barry E.C. Fellinger, a mustang officer who had been a Staff NCO for over 15 years. The Platoon Sgt. was SSgt John Rwznicki.

I quickly rose to Fire team leader, 1st Squad Leader and to Right Guide. The new Platoon Sgt. was John Harmon. Before long, Lt. Fellinger was promoted to Captain and to Executive Officer and we were told that our new Platoon Leader would be Lt. Frank M. Izenour, Jr. The entire platoon was thrilled over the announcement.

Lt. Izenour was tall, about 6'2". Sgt. Harmon was short by Marine standards. Harmon was also a "salty short-timer" who was married to a Woman Marine Officer with a new baby. His "Espirit De Corps" was fading fast! On one trip to Camp David, Harmon did something that I learned to avoid... He really irritated Lt. Izenour. To this day, I don't know what Harmon did, exactly, but I do know that it was the last thing he ever did as Platoon Sgt. for "Ike" as we affectionately called Lt. Izenour. Frank strolled down the hall from Room One at Camp David and handed me a black Leather Belt, worn only by Platoon Sergeants and Officers. He said, "Here, put this on, you're the new Platoon Sergeant". I looked him squarely in the eye and said..."Yes, Sir." No questions were asked or answered about the circumstances surrounding my promotion. I became the new Platoon Sergeant of 2nd Platoon.

"Ike" was a real pistol! He had a great sense of humor and a tame ego. Frank was soon promoted to Captain and began billing himself as a "Captain of Marines". We all enjoyed his new title, as he did his rank.

After all, we were the Marines of whom he was the Captain.

In a very short time, the 2nd Platoon began to shape up and gained a solid reputation as a crack unit, second only to Lt. Sheldon J. Bathurst's Silent Drill Team. Sheldon J. Bathurst later retired as a Colonel.

Every other month, we would rotate with the 3d Platoon for duty at Camp David. Frank loved "The Hill" as we called Camp #3. An avid skier, Frank alternated liberty with me when the President wasn't in residence.

It was now nearing the end of 1968 and President Johnson was ready to leave office. On his last trip to the hill, LBJ and his family said their last goodbyes to the senior people. I recall Lucy and Linda Johnson both flirting with Frank as LBJ called out, "Come on girls, you're in love with enough Marines already". (Captain Chuck Robb would become LBJ's son-in-law very shortly thereafter).

By no means did Frank consider himself a "Ladies man", but rather a strong silent type. On a few occasions, Frank and I would double date. (I always had to fix him up) The only complaint the girls had was..."He's just too much of a gentleman". Nice work if you can get it!

Although Frank was only 26 years old at the time, he was prematurely bald. I suspect it really didn't bother him as much as he pretended. Overall, Ike was unflappable, a real easy going Gyrene Gentleman.

1969 was a New Year with a new President. A President who's son-in law was the namesake of Camp David. We spent a lot of long weekends at Camp David that winter. Often Frank and I would check posts together around the three mile perimeter of Camp David at all hours of the day and night. Frank set a great example for all of us. He didn't just sleep all night while I got up to check posts at 2:00 a.m. No matter how cold it was or what the hour; Frank was up and on the job, giving encouragement to the men. The all night duty wasn't so bad when the officers were braving the elements along with the men.

One bitterly cold day, Frank and I went on a routine visit to the Field House that served as a storage facility for Camp David. We found an old snow sled and since we had two or three feet of snow on the ground, we decided to check posts via sled. What a ball! That is until we got going too fast down a hill and "Fearless Leader" steered us into a tree. Poor Frank, he was in the front. All I got was the back of his bald head against my chin; he got what was probably a 100-year-old Sycamore tree. It was no contest. Frank was a mess; he looked like he had just fought Muhammad Ali. No more sled trips that year.

As the year wore on, the news of former President Dwight D. Eisenhower's failing health became increasingly grim. When I was in the 1st grade, Eisenhower was President. The heart attack he suffered at that time made national headlines. Our class wrote him a get-well letter. We received a very cordial thank you letter from Mrs. Mamie Eisenhower. Little did I know that several years later I would be selected as one of the Marines to serve on President Eisenhower's funeral detail.

We began practicing "Operation Abilene" about six weeks prior to Eisenhower's death. The detail consisted of one officer from each branch of the service, and one enlisted man from each branch of the service. Frank Izenour and I were on the same detail. One day in March 1969 while at Camp David, Frank Izenour called me at Room 10 at BOQ with the news...President Eisenhower had died. We piled into a bus and raced back to the Barracks at 8th & I in Washington to change into our ceremonial dress blues and drove straight to Gawler's Funeral Home to assume the "Deathwatch".

The next day the late President's body was moved to the Bethlehem Chapel of the Washington Cathedral. Each branch of the service served a seemingly endless shift that actually only lasted an hour. The duty was tough. Standing at attention, walking in slow motion, everything was in slow motion. A nod from Frank, not visible to the crowd, would signal us to move slowly to Parade Rest, then back to attention with the same nod. I will never forget my feelings as I slowly marched, "Deathwatch" style, past President and Mrs. Nixon and their family, Mamie Eisenhower and the late President's brother. I was afraid that I would trip or somehow make a mistake. Frank, on the other hand, appeared to be as cool as a cucumber.

Frank's father was a retired Major General in the Army...The uncanny and amazing irony was that Frank looked like the spitting image of President Dwight D. Eisenhower as a young officer. One young army Sgt. on the detail came up to Frank and noticing the physical resemblance and identical sounding name, asked, "Sir, are you any relation to General Eisenhower? The wrong choice of words! Frank answered without hesitation in his very dry humor, "Yes; he's my Dad". The poor Sgt. turned pale and almost passed out! Frank just walked away and winked at us as he passed.

As our shift repeated itself, the more confident we became. From the Washington Cathedral, the body was taken to the Rotunda of the Capitol to lie in state. Frank and I stood guard over the President's casket while such notables as President Richard M. Nixon, Charles DeGaulle, and a host of foreign dignitaries paid their final respects to the legendary General of World War II and former President.

The fact that President Eisenhower was buried in his uniform and former "Ike Jacket" presented a slight problem. The U.S. Army had discontinued the issuance of Tropical shirts. Only the Marine Corps still issued them as part of the uniform. A runner was sent to the Marine Barracks at 8th & I to procure a "very small" Tropical shirt. A young, slightly built Corporal volunteered one of his, not knowing the purpose for which it would be used. The Corporal asked, "When will I get it back"? The runner replied "we're going to bury him (Eisenhower) in it." So, underneath the famous "Ike Battle Jacket", one would find a shirt with the faint stitched outline of a Marine Corporal's chevrons.

The body of the late President was placed on a train en route to Abilene, Kansas. Accompanying the body was Corporal Rich Porter. Frank and I, along with Sgt. Ernie Richardson of 3rd Platoon and 30 or so officers and men on the "Deathwatch" flew to Abilene via Military Air Transport. The officers were billeted in a nearby motel, while the local High School Gymnasium served as "Home" for the enlisted men. We had a long wait for the train to catch up, so Frank and I decided to see the town of Abilene. For some reason that I fail to recall, the town of Abilene was closed! Frank and I were bound and determined to have a cold beer. The only place in town that was open was the local VFW club. We joined! That was the first and last time I (and probably Frank) ever set foot in a VFW Club. No offense meant to the VFW, it just wasn't good timing on our part. Although we were both Viet Nam veterans, that didn't really qualify as a "War" to the regular patrons of that particular club. WWI, WW II, Korea, maybe. But not Viet Nam. Pretty soon night fell and not long after, so did we. Frank was lucky; he didn't have as far to walk.

Bright and early the next morning we met the train at the station. The entourage was there and the parade was forming. As the train pulled into the station, a very hesitant Frank Izenour informed me that only he and I would be assuming the next "Deathwatch" shift due to limited space on the train car that carried the casket. Frank and I ceremonially positioned ourselves at opposite ends of the casket. How much time elapsed, I don't know? Then it happened... A small party of people, including Mamie Eisenhower boarded the train and approached the casket. Frank and I were standing at attention with our head and eyes straight to the front. Frank and I had a routine worked out. We would stare holes in each other's foreheads. Slowly, one of the men in the party began to fold back the flag draped over the casket. My fears were immediately confirmed, as the side latches were unfastened. The top half of the casket (facing Frank) was opened, exposing the frail, lifeless body of the late President. The urge was too strong for both of us...Frank's eyes widened like saucers with curiosity, so did mine. We both looked down! It was shocking and unforgettable! The curled hands, folded across the chest looked more like a monkey's than a General's. Eisenhower only weighed about 120 pounds when he died, so he had withered away quite a bit.

It never came up between Frank and me until 18 years later when we both admitted to each other that we had looked. We both knew it, but never talked about it.

After the funeral, Frank Izenour was promoted to Executive Officer, reporting to Major Frank Breth. Major Breth would later retire as a Brigadier General. Replacing Captain Izenour as Platoon Leader of 2nd Platoon was First Lieutenant Peter Pace. Lt. Pace was a graduate of the U.S. Naval Academy and had just returned from Viet Nam. Following in Frank Izenour's footsteps was no small task as Frank was extremely popular with the troops. However, Lt. Pace soon gained the respect of all the troops and was a top-notch officer. Before too long, Lt. Pace was assigned to replace Lt. Thomas Esslinger as Platoon Leader of the Special Ceremonial Platoon, which included the Silent Drill Team, Color Guard, and the Body Bearers. In 1988, Peter Pace, by then a Colonel, returned to the Marine Barracks at 8th & I, in Washington, D.C. as the Commanding Officer. Peter Pace later became a Four Star General and Commander in Chief of the U.S. Southern Command, reporting directly to the Secretary of Defense. In August, 2001, President George W. Bush nominated General Peter Pace to the position of Vice Chairman of the Joint Chiefs of Staff. After confirmation by the Senate, General Peter Pace became the highest ranking Marine in Marine Corps history. In April 2005, President George W. Bush nominated General Pace to become the Chairman of the Joint Chiefs of Staff. General Pace was sworn in on 30 September 2005 as the first Marine to become the Chairman of the Joint Chiefs of Staff. I had the privilege to attend the swearing in ceremony.

Despite the urging of First Sergeant Leland "Crow" Crawford to refuse my orders to go back to Viet Nam and remain at the barracks until my release date of 15 March 1970, I left Washington D.C. in January 1970. In February 1970, I was released early from active duty and returned home to Ft. Lauderdale, Florida. In September 1970, I left Florida for California. The week after I left, my Mother got a phone call from Frank Izenour; he was in town and wanted to see me. Lousy timing!

Frank had received orders to go back to Viet Nam. Although wounded the first time around, Frank was luckier on his second tour. Saigon in 1971, when a Dong was still worth a Dong! (The Dong was the monetary unit of the Republic of South Viet Nam.)

Frank and I missed connections on his return to the States. I would call Frank or he would call me every November 10th on the Marine Corps Birthday. In the last few years we would call more often, maybe it was the AT&T ads, I don't know...

Frank talked about his retirement almost each and every call. In April 1988, I called Frank to let him know I would be attending a meeting in Washington, D.C.

Frank's office was in Crystal City, just across from National Airport. On April 11, 1988 I waited with anticipation for my old friend whom I hadn't seen for 19 years. The elevator opened and down the hall strode the same Frank Izenour, tall, still slim, and relatively unchanged in 19 years. What a great reunion! We sat and talked for five hours and ten beers! Frank invited me to come out to his house and meet his family. I had to conduct a Seminar and wasn't able to break away, however, I assured him that I would be back in Washington again soon. I did return the next month, but Frank got lost so we missed each other again. Oh well, I knew we'd get together again soon. We talked a few more times after his retirement in June, mostly about his progress in his consulting work.

I missed the usual November 10th call, but made a follow up call a month or so later. On Friday, December 16th, 1988 Frank called and was very excited about a new book he was writing. That book won't be finished now... Frank M. Izenour, Jr. died late in the evening on Friday, December 16th of a massive heart attack. He left a widow, Susan, and two young children Chris and Katy. Frank Izenour was also survived by his parents, Maj. Gen. Frank M. Izenour, Sr. and his mother, Billie.

Colonel Peter Pace, Commanding Officer of the Marine Barracks 8th & I Streets, Washington D.C. presided over the funeral of his old friend Lt. Col. Frank M. Izenour, Jr. and presented the United States Flag , on behalf of a grateful nation, to Frank's widow, Susan Izenour.

I didn't find out about Frank's death until March 13, 1989 when making a routine call to just say hello. It has taken me a year to be able to put these words on paper so his family would have some knowledge of Frank's "Glory Days" at the Marine Barracks, 8th & I Streets, Washington, D.C.

Frank Izenour will be greatly missed by his family and friends. He was a great Marine and a great man.

Here's to you, Frank. Lest we forget...